How To

CLONE

A SHEEP

How To
CLONE
A SHEEP

By HAZEL RICHARDSON

Illustrated by
Andy Cooke

FRANKLIN WATTS
A Division of Scholastic Inc.
New York Toronto London Auckland Sydney
Mexico City New Delhi Hong Kong
Danbury, Connecticut

For Oliver and Thomas

First published 1999 by Oxford University Press
Great Clarendon Street, Oxford OX2 6DP

First American edition 2001 by Franklin Watts
A Division of Scholastic Inc.
90 Sherman Turnpike
Danbury, CT 06816

Catalog details are available from the Library of Congress
Cataloging-in-Publication Data

ISBN 0-531-14645-6 (lib. bdg.) 0-531-16200-1 (pbk.)

Printed in China

Contents

HOW TO CLONE A SHEEP

On July 5, 1996, something happened that would change the course of human history. This was more amazing than people landing on the moon. The news spread around the world within hours. Some people were delighted and excited. Other people were horrified.

What had happened?

A lamb named Dolly had been born in a shed in Scotland.

It might seem silly that the birth of a lamb could make millions of people excited or scared, but this was a very special lamb. Dolly was an exact copy, or clone, of another sheep. It was the first time scientists successfully cloned an adult animal. It meant people might soon be able to clone any other animal—even a human—if we want to!

In this book, you will learn all about

- ◎ what DNA and genes are
- ◎ how embryos grow into animals
- ◎ what cloning is
- ◎ why cloning is so difficult to do
- ◎ why we can probably clone humans if we want to
- ◎ why cloning scares some people
- ◎ the scientists who discovered how to clone animals
- ◎ how you can clone plants at home

CHAPTER ONE

WHAT IS A CLONE?

A clone is an exact copy of a living thing. Scientists have been able to clone plants and bacteria (germs) for a long time. Now that Dolly has been born, we can clone adult animals and probably even humans, too!

Making a copy of a living thing is much more difficult than making a copy of something that isn't living, like a mountain bike. For many years, people have tried to make robots that look and behave like humans. In science-fiction films and TV shows, we often see androids—creatures that are part human and part robot. But in real life, scientists haven't been very successful. Robots still look like hunks of metal. They don't move like we do, and they don't think like we do.

Robots don't look like living things because they are built out of materials that are not living. Living things are built out of tiny building blocks called cells. Scientists can't make their own cells yet.

Robots don't behave like living things because they are programmed (given instructions about how to behave). Robot computer programs are very complicated, but not a millionth as complicated as what living things are programmed by—DNA.

But I'm not programmed like a computer!

Believe it or not, you are! Everything about you depends on the instructions you get from DNA. This means that if we could copy your DNA, we could make another human that looks just like you! This person would be your clone.

DNA ....

What is DNA?

◎ DNA is a very complicated chemical called deoxyribonucleic acid. Scientists use the abbreviation "DNA" so they don't have to write its full name out all the time.

◎ DNA looks like a long, spiraling ladder. It carries a secret code that the body can read. This code tells living things what they will look like, what they should eat, and how they should grow.

◎ Everything about how you look is determined by what the code in DNA says.

There are millions of copies of the DNA code inside you. You can go and find them if you shrink to a tiny size and go inside your body!

The Incredible Journey

There are things going on inside your body that you wouldn't believe. Inside you are highways, factories, and even an army that kills invaders!

Here you are on your arm. It looks like a forest with tall hair-trees towering above you. Go and look in a pore. It looks like a deep well going down as far as you can see. What happens if you fall in?

pore

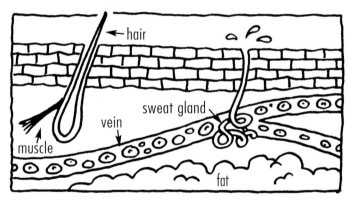

hair

sweat gland

vein

muscle

fat

Now that you're under your skin, you can see how much is going on. There's a sweat gland, squirting out liquid. There's a muscle, making the hair stand on end when you get cold. And here's what looks like a road, full of red liquid. This is your blood. If you shrink even more, you can go for a ride in it!

You can't usually see these tiny things in your blood. They are red blood cells. They're round and have a dent in the middle. They are used to carry oxygen from your lungs to the rest of your body. You're now small enough to sit in the dent, but hang on—it's a bumpy ride!

As you ride along, you notice other cells. These are white blood cells. They move along by stretching parts of themselves out and pulling the rest along. They are a loyal army of cells that seek out and eat any germs that get inside you.

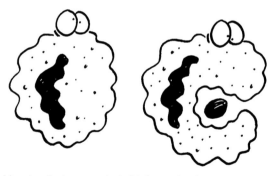

White blood cells have a dark blob inside them. As you rush along the blood road, you see that the sides of the road are made of blocklike cells. These also have dark blobs inside them. In fact, every cell you see has a dark blob—except for the red blood cells.

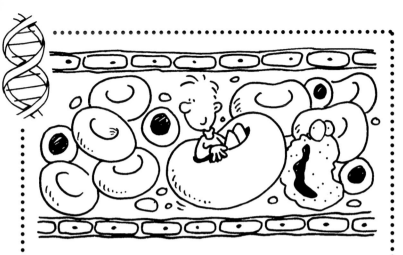

These dark blobs are very, very important. They are called cell nuclei (nucleus if there's just one of them). If you get off your red blood cell and shrink a bit more, you can go inside one of the cells and see what they do.

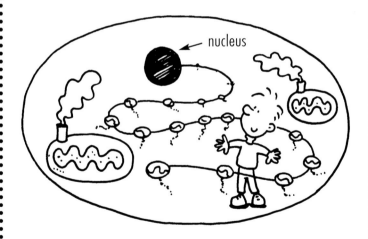

nucleus

Here you are inside a cell. It's just like a factory. There's a conveyor belt putting things together, and the weird sausage-shaped blobs are little power stations.

nucleus

Here's a close-up of the nucleus in a cell that's about to divide. Inside it are what look like lots of very long, coiled-up pieces of string. These are called chromosomes. Chromosomes are made up of DNA. Every cell in your body has chromosomes, except red blood cells. Red blood cells need extra space inside them to carry oxygen around your body.

What Has DNA and What Doesn't? ....

Every living thing on Earth has some DNA inside it. Simple living things, such as bacteria, can carry all their DNA on only one chromosome. They have only a small amount of DNA because they don't need many instructions about how to grow. More complicated animals and plants have lots of chromosomes. Humans have forty-six chromosomes in most cells in their bodies. You need this much DNA because there are so many different parts of you that need instructions: your hair and eye color; how to grow bones, your heart, your liver, and all your other organs; how to move—and much more!

Here's what human chromosomes look like:

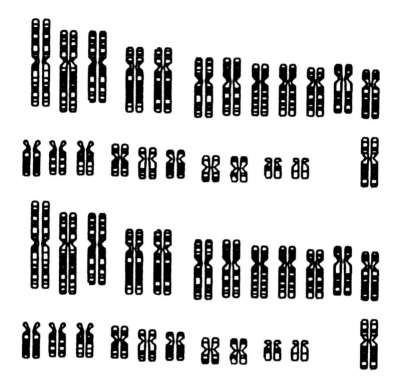

Do you notice something strange in this picture? It looks like there are two copies of each chromosome. But why would you need two copies?

You have two copies of the DNA instructions because you get one set from your mother and one set from your father.

CHAPTER TWO

HOW BABIES GROW

All animals, including humans, reproduce by joining a cell from the father, called a sperm cell, with a cell from the mother, called an egg. These are very special cells because they are made with just one copy of the DNA code—only 23 chromosomes. When the egg and sperm cell join, it is called fertilization.

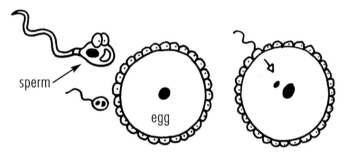

sperm

egg

The 23 chromosomes from the sperm join the 23 chromosomes from the egg to make 46 chromosomes. Once the egg cell has all 46 chromosomes, it has all the instructions it needs to develop into a new human being, so it starts growing.

For a fertilized egg to become a new human being, it needs to grow arms, legs, a head—everything. This takes a long time. First, the cell splits in two, and into two again, until it is a ball of cells. Then something amazing happens. The cells read their DNA code, and each one takes on a job to do in the new body.

Once the cells have taken on the jobs they're going to do, they look at their DNA for instructions on how to do that job. Then they become the kind of cell that they are going to be in the new body. The ball of cells starts to grow arms, legs, a heart, lungs, kidneys, and all the other parts that you have. This developing ball of cells is called a blastula.

It takes about ten weeks for the egg to grow into an embryo that looks like a human baby. But even this embryo is very tiny. It has to grow inside the mother for another seven months or so before it can face life outside on its own.

Before we knew all this, people used to have some funny ideas about how babies were made.

17

Fertilization Facts
Part 1

Ancient Greece, around 350 B.C.

This is Aristotle, one of the most important scientists of all time. People around him are beginning to ask questions about why animals, plants, and humans look like they do. Aristotle's many books on this subject will be used thousands of years after his death.

Today, he's trying to figure out how babies are made. He's busy breaking open hens' eggs and looking at the baby chicks inside. This seems like a cruel thing to do, but it is the only way he can find out how babies grow.

He notices that at first, the unborn chick just looks like a tiny blob. It grows its head, legs, and wings before it hatches. He guesses that a tiny part of the egg could grow into a whole new animal.

Aristotle is right, but not everyone agrees with him. Most men like to think that women just give the baby food to grow, and the baby is made by the man. A Roman named Seneca says that every sperm has a tiny human inside it. It is so tiny that it can't be seen, and all it has to do is grow bigger once it has food from the mother. He says that it doesn't need to make arms, legs, and a head—they're already there.

Who was right?

Be a Genetic Scientist

WATCH AN EMBRYO GROWING

It isn't easy (or kind) to watch a chicken embryo growing like Aristotle did. The eggs you buy in the grocery store are unfertilized and would never turn into chickens. But you can watch an embryo growing very easily if you collect some frog eggs.

WHAT YOU'LL NEED
- ◎ some frog eggs from a pond (you'll only find them in the spring, in a jellylike mass of little black dots)
- ◎ a net
- ◎ a few glass jars filled with pond water

WHAT TO DO
1. In early spring, find a pond with frog eggs. (A science teacher at school should be able to help you.) If you look closely at them, you will see that the eggs are round and whitish clear, with a black dot in the middle. This dot is the nucleus, which contains DNA for building the frog.

2. Collect some frog eggs using the net, then put them into the jar filled with pond water and take it home.

3. Keep the frog eggs in a cool, safe place and watch what happens to them. They won't need any food, just water.

WHAT HAPPENS?
You will see the frog eggs splitting up and growing into tadpoles.

Mommy!

Please be kind to animals. When you have grown your tadpoles, take them back to the pond so they can grow into frogs. Once the eggs have become tadpoles, they need food from the pond or they will die.

Spying on Cells ....

After the microscope was invented in 1609, scientists were able to see cells and the nuclei inside them. They watched egg cells splitting into two new cells and growing. But they still believed Seneca's idea about how animals are made. The first scientists who looked at sperm drew them with a little man inside each one. They were sure they could see them!

By the end of the nineteenth century, scientists had finally realized that a single fertilized egg cell grows into a completely new animal made up of millions of cells. This raised a lot of questions.

The only answers people could think of were...

It sounded sensible. After all, polar bears *were* white, and they all lived in the same place. Grizzly bears were all brown, and they lived in the same place. So animals and plants must look like they do just because of where they live.

This answer made sense, but it was wrong. When polar bears in a zoo have babies, they are still white— even though they no longer need to be camouflaged against the ice. A grizzly bear that lives in the snow doesn't have white babies. There was something in animals and plants that told their children to look just like them. What could it be?

Then Charles Darwin came along.

Fertilization Facts
Part II
England, 1859

Leave this to me!

In 1859, Charles Darwin published one of the most famous books ever written: *On the Origin of Species by Means of Natural Selection*. This book caused a lot of trouble. Before Darwin came along, most people believed in the Biblical story of creation, in which God made every creature on Earth. Other scientists had proposed the idea that animals had changed through time, or evolved, in some way. Darwin and some other scientists discovered something very important. They found fossils of animals that no longer existed. They noticed that some of these extinct animals looked like animals that *were* still alive. Darwin figured out how animals could change from one type of animal into another type over thousands or millions of years. He developed a new theory of evolution.

People found it very hard to believe Darwin's theory that humans had evolved from apes. They were shocked and horrified. Religious people laughed at him—and got very angry.

Because of Darwin's ideas and research, scientists now believe that life on Earth started off as simple bacteria. These changed into more complicated animals, which eventually evolved into fish. Some fish evolved into animals that could live on land. These evolved into dinosaurs and mammals. The dinosaurs evolved into birds, and the mammals evolved into the many different species that we see today. Darwin said that all the animals in a species (type) have slight differences between them. You can see this if you look at your friends and family. You are all humans, but you all look slightly different. Some giraffes, for example, have slightly longer necks than others. Some lions can run faster than others. Sometimes animals have a slight difference that makes them more likely to survive.

Giraffes with longer necks are more likely to survive because they can reach higher branches to eat the leaves.

The longer-necked giraffes have babies who also have longer necks. Soon, all giraffes will have longer necks than they used to. The giraffes have evolved.

Even though Darwin figured out that animals could change, he couldn't figure out why the children of long-necked giraffes also had long necks.

Babies look like their parents because the blood from the mother gets mixed up with the blood from the father.

Wrong again!

Keeping It in the Family ....

Darwin's cousin, Francis Galton, thought the theory of evolution was nonsense. He did an experiment on rabbits to prove Darwin wrong. (Nice cousin, eh?) He took a white female rabbit and mated her with a white male rabbit. Then he took some blood from a black rabbit and injected it into the white female rabbit. Next, he waited for the white rabbit's babies to be born, to see what color they were.

Were the babies:
A. white
B. black

The baby rabbits were all white, even though their mother had been injected with black rabbit blood.

So, Galton knew that how you look has nothing to do with your mom and dad's blood. The reason why we look like our parents remained a mystery.

CHAPTER THREE

GENIUS GENES

It's a shame Darwin didn't get to meet a monk named Gregor Mendel. Mendel discovered why babies look like their parents at the same time that Darwin was asking his questions.

Fertilization Facts Part III
Austria, 1860

This is Gregor Mendel. Right now he's not very happy. He wants to be a scientist, but he doesn't have the support he needs to go to school.

I'll show you all! I'm going to grow peas and become rich and famous!

Mendel decides to become a monk. Being a monk gives him lots of time to work in the monastery gardens growing plants. Soon he notices something strange about pea plants: some have smooth seeds, and some have wrinkled ones.

Peas are the seeds of pea plants. When a pea is planted, it grows into a new plant. Just like animals, baby plants are made from a special female egg cell and a special male pollen cell. If you look at a flower, you can find these special cells.

Most flowers look like this:

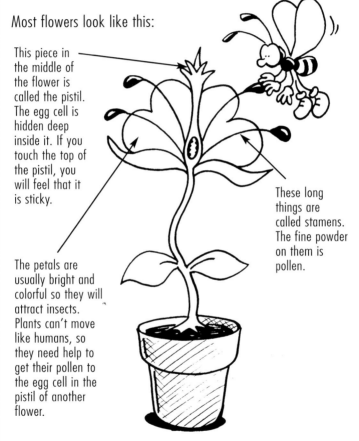

This piece in the middle of the flower is called the pistil. The egg cell is hidden deep inside it. If you touch the top of the pistil, you will feel that it is sticky.

These long things are called stamens. The fine powder on them is pollen.

The petals are usually bright and colorful so they will attract insects. Plants can't move like humans, so they need help to get their pollen to the egg cell in the pistil of another flower.

Usually, insects pick up some pollen when they visit a flower. They fly to another flower, and some of the pollen gets stuck onto the sticky tip of the pistil. The pollen cells dig a tunnel to get to the egg.

Scientists can make flowers have babies by taking some of the pollen from one flower and placing it on the pistil of another flower. This is called cross-pollinating. Mendel discovered that he could cross a wrinkly-pea plant with a smooth-pea plant to see what kind of peas the baby plants would make. He found that all the baby plants made smooth peas. What had happened to the wrinkles?

Very curious, Mendel decided to see what would happen when these smooth-pea baby plants had baby plants of their own. Some of these new plants made wrinkly peas—the wrinkliness had come back! What in the world was going on?

Mendel came up with an explanation. He said that each pea plant had instructions inside it, telling it which kind of pea to make. He called these instructions "factors." Today we call them genes. Each pea plant gets two gene instructions about which kind of pea to make—one from its mother and one from its father plant.

Make smooth peas!

Make wrinkly peas!

The smooth-pea gene is dominant. The wrinkly-pea gene is weaker, or recessive.

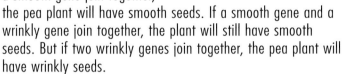

I'm the strongest!

Errrgh!

So, if a smooth gene and a smooth gene join together, the pea plant will have smooth seeds. If a smooth gene and a wrinkly gene join together, the plant will still have smooth seeds. But if two wrinkly genes join together, the pea plant will have wrinkly seeds.

You can see on the chart below how this explains Mendel's results.

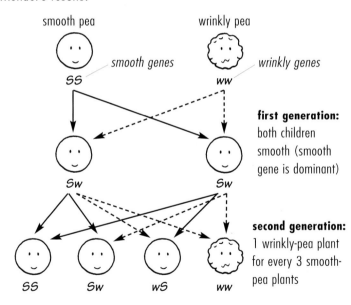

smooth pea

wrinkly pea

smooth genes

wrinkly genes

SS

ww

first generation: both children smooth (smooth gene is dominant)

Sw

Sw

second generation: 1 wrinkly-pea plant for every 3 smooth-pea plants

SS

Sw

wS

ww

Genes determine more than wrinkliness or smoothness. Everything about a pea plant is controlled by genes. It's the same for people.

Be a Genetic Scientist
MAP OUT YOUR OWN GENES

There are genes for all kinds of things. For instance, did you know there is a gene for whether or not your ear has a big lobe?

lobe   no lobe

You can draw a chart like the one below for yourself, showing who in your family has earlobes and who doesn't.

☐ males with no earlobes   ■ males with earlobes
○ females with no earlobes   ● females with earlobes

GRANDPARENTS:

PARENTS:

BROTHERS AND
SISTERS:

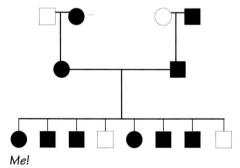

Me!

How Do I Get Genes from My Parents? . . . .

Remember the chromosomes inside you? There are two copies of each one. One of the copies comes from your father, and one comes from your mother. Each chromosome carries the genes for different things about you. Because there are two copies, the cells have to decide which gene they are going to listen to. Sometimes they listen to both, and then you look like a mix of the two genes.

The joining of two recessive genes is what happened in Mendel's wrinkly-pea plants.

Unfortunately, when Mendel tried to tell other scientists about his pea plants, everyone ignored him.

Mendel soon gave up and started working on hawkweed instead. He got into a bitter argument with the government about his monastery's taxes, smoked twenty cigars a day, and developed heart disease. He spent his last days sitting on a couch with his feet in bandages, suffering from edema. (Edema is a horrible disease that makes you swell up.) Mendel died in 1884, a very unhappy and bitter man.

Mendel's work was discovered sixteen years after his death by three scientists who were arguing about who discovered dominant and recessive genes first. It turned out Mendel had beaten them all to it!

CHAPTER FOUR

THE LINK BETWEEN GENES AND DNA

By 1900, we knew that genes make us look the way we do. But scientists didn't know where these genes were. What were they made of?

We now know that genes are made of DNA, which is found in long strings called chromosomes. But this was discovered completely by accident...

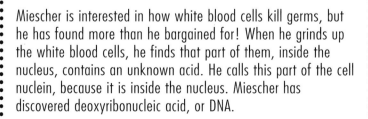

The Search for Genes
Part I
Switzerland, 1869

Here's Frederick Miescher. He's taking pus out of a bandage used on an amputated leg. (Ugh! What a job!)

Miescher is interested in how white blood cells kill germs, but he has found more than he bargained for! When he grinds up the white blood cells, he finds that part of them, inside the nucleus, contains an unknown acid. He calls this part of the cell nuclein, because it is inside the nucleus. Miescher has discovered deoxyribonucleic acid, or DNA.

DNA, a Marvelous Mystery ....

Miescher had no idea what DNA was for. At that time, nobody had seen chromosomes inside cells, and nobody knew about Mendel's amazing discoveries of how babies look like their parents. Miescher continued working with DNA, though, and found a very important clue: sperm were made up of DNA and very little else. Could there be a link, he wondered, between DNA and how babies look?

The Search for Genes
Part II
Germany, 1888

Here's Walther Flemming, looking at cells as they divide. He sees some long stringy things in the nucleus. He calls the stringy things chromosomes, but thinks nothing of them.

Chromosome Contents ....

In 1907, Thomas Hunt Morgan first noticed the link between genes and chromosomes. He wasn't convinced by Mendel's gene theories. He decided to breed fruit flies to see if Mendel's ideas about genes were true. They were! He concluded that the only part of the cell that could contain genes had to be a long, stringy thing—a chromosome.

The problem now was that chromosomes are not just made up of DNA. They have a coating of protein around them. Scientists were puzzled. They couldn't figure out which carried the gene instructions—the protein or the DNA. Then, an important experiment with some nasty germs gave us the answer...

The Search for Genes Part III
England, 1944

This is Fred Griffith. He's working on some bacteria called pneumococci (pronounced "nu-mo-COKS-eye"). Some of these bacteria cause the disease pneumonia, while others don't.

Bacteria don't have babies like animals and plants. When they want to make more of themselves, they get thinner in the middle and split into two. This makes two new bacteria, each of which is exactly like the parent. Because the two new bacteria are identical, they are clones.

Be a Genetic Scientist

CLONE YOUR OWN BACTERIA

You can see how a single bacterium splits up and makes copies of itself in an experiment using Jell-O™. Have an adult help you.

WHAT YOU'LL NEED
◎ some Jell-O mix
◎ two old yogurt containers
◎ a toothpick (plastic is best)
◎ plastic wrap

WHAT TO DO
1. Sterilize one of the yogurt containers by soaking it in boiling water.
2. Mix up a small amount of Jell-O according to the instructions on the box. Pour it into the yogurt container, but not to the very top. Cover it immediately with plastic wrap.
3. When the Jell-O has solidified, peel back a little bit of the plastic wrap. Rub one finger around your gums and teeth and then press it against the Jell-O.
4. Cover the container again and leave it in a warm place (where no one will find it and throw it out).
5. Check the Jell-O every day to see what is growing on it. Soon, you will see little blobs on the Jell-O. These are bacteria from your mouth. You can clone these.

Ick! It's getting all furry!

6. Sterilize the other yogurt container.
7. Mix up more Jell-O, pour it into the container to solidify, and cover it with plastic wrap just like you did before. (Make sure there is an air space between the Jell-O and the plastic wrap.)
8. Sterilize the toothpick.
9. Carefully open the container with the bacteria inside and stick the toothpick into a lump of bacteria. This should pick up a few bacteria. Touch the toothpick onto the newly made Jell-O and cover it up.
10. Leave it in a safe, warm place and see what happens.

BE CAREFUL
Bacteria cause diseases and
can be dangerous!
Throw away the containers and the
Jell-O when you finish this experiment.
ALWAYS wash your hands after you've
touched the experiment.

WHAT HAPPENS?
The few bacteria that you pick up on the toothpick divide up to make many more bacteria. These are all clones of the bacteria you had in your mouth. (Yuck! Now you know why you should brush your teeth.)

The Search for Genes
Part IV
Back to England, 1944

Fred Griffiths found that the bacteria that caused pneumonia always made new bacteria that caused pneumonia. Bacteria that didn't cause the disease always made new bacteria that didn't cause the disease. Griffiths knew that causing a disease is something that the bacteria inherit—just like you inherit eye color and other traits from your parents.

Griffiths wanted to know which part of the bacteria carried the disease-causing genes. So he did a really nasty experiment on some rabbits. He killed some disease bacteria by heating them up. Then he injected them into a rabbit. The rabbit didn't get sick.

Then he mixed up the dead bacteria with some healthy bacteria. When he injected the mixture, the rabbits got sick. The healthy bacteria were following instructions from the dead bacteria. All Griffiths had to do was find out which part of the dead bacteria carried the instructions. He broke open the bacteria and separated them into all their parts. He tried the experiment again and again until he found the one part of the dead bacteria that made the healthy bacteria turn bad. This part was the chromosome.

Finally Finding Genes........................

Griffiths was convinced that genes were carried on the DNA part of the chromosome, but he couldn't prove it. Other scientists thought the protein coating on the chromosomes carried the genes instead. It was left to Oswald Avery to save the day...

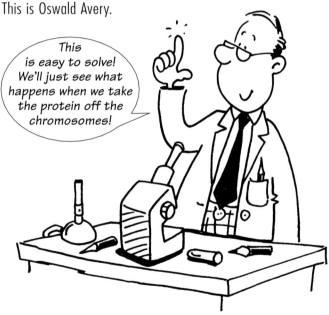

The Search for Genes Part V
The United States, 1944

This is Oswald Avery.

This is easy to solve! We'll just see what happens when we take the protein off the chromosomes!

With this experiment, Avery proves that the protein doesn't have anything to do with genes. The way every living thing looks depends on the DNA in its chromosomes.

CHAPTER FIVE

CRACKING THE CODE

Once scientists knew that genes were carried on chromosomes made of DNA, the race was on to find out how the cells read the genes. Genes work by telling the cells which proteins to make. You've probably heard of protein in food, but believe it or not, there are hundreds of types of protein—including proteins that your body makes. This type of protein makes you look the way you do.

Here are some important proteins made by cells inside your body:

- ◎ muscle protein
- ◎ hemoglobin, which carries oxygen around your body inside red blood cells
- ◎ enzymes, which break down food inside you
- ◎ keratin, which makes hair and nails
- ◎ collagen, which makes your skin elastic

How can a long, stringy piece of DNA tell a stomach cell to make a protein that digests food?
To find this out, scientists had to see how DNA was put together. The first scientist to find this out would know exactly how genes worked—and would become rich and famous!

The DNA Race

Here we are in the 1950s, ready for an exciting race to see which scientist is the first to figure out what DNA looks like. The winner will receive a Nobel Prize and lots of money. Let's take a look at the lineup.

First is Linus Pauling, the favorite to win the race. He has already won the Nobel Prize and has figured out what proteins look like. They are a twisty spiral shape called a helix.

Next is Rosalind Franklin, a clever woman who knows how to take X-ray pictures of DNA, which should help her. But she might be slowed down because she's one of the few women in a university dominated by men.

Maurice Wilkins is the second favorite. He has some X-ray pictures of DNA that should help him find out how it works.

Next is James Watson, a young American who wants to win the Nobel Prize and is inspired by a scientist he works with, Francis Crick.

Finally, we have Francis Crick, the surprise outsider. He has lots of good ideas, but isn't very good at sitting down and working at them.

And they're off!

Linus Pauling takes the early lead by announcing that DNA is a helix, just like some proteins. But he stumbles at the first hurdle when he claims DNA has three strands twisted around each other. (It actually has two.) Too bad!

There are four runners in the race now. Maurice Wilkins is slightly ahead, because he knows how to take pictures of DNA. He teams up with Rosalind Franklin, who can also take pictures of DNA. Wilkins and Franklin pull further into the lead.

James Watson and Francis Crick are next. But they don't really get anywhere because they do most of their research by sitting in a coffee shop trying to build little models out of wire.

But, what's this? Wilkins and Franklin have had a fight! Franklin is starting to work on her own, and she's doing very well. She's pulling ahead of Wilkins, who is annoyed. He's slowing down to talk to Watson and Crick.

Wilkins shows Watson and Crick a picture that Franklin took—without asking her! Is this allowed? It must be, because Wilkins hasn't been disqualified.

There's another surprise! Two new people are on the race track: Erwin Chargaff and Jerry Donahue. They're talking to Watson and Crick, telling them how the two strands of DNA join together.

This is a close race! Franklin is writing up her results. Can she get them published first? Oh, no! Watson and Crick put on a sudden burst of speed. They build a model. It looks accurate. Watson is getting his sister to write up his results. He's mailed it off.

Watson and Crick win the race! Franklin limps home in second place, closely followed by Wilkins, in third.

Looking Inside DNA.............................

James Watson and Francis Crick went on to win the Nobel Prize for discovering the structure of DNA. Maurice Wilkins shared the prize with them because of the help he had given. Poor Rosalind Franklin died before the prize was given. Dead people can't be awarded the Nobel Prize.

Crick and Watson's model looked like this.

DNA looks like a twisty ladder. There are two sides, with rungs joining them together. This is called a double helix.
Believe it or not, those rungs carry all the genes you need to

make you look exactly the way you do. Here's how it works. There are four special molecules, called bases, in DNA. The rungs are made up of two bases joined together in the middle. The four bases are called

- adenine
- thymine
- cytosine
- guanine

To make things easier, scientists call them A, T, C, and G.

A always joins with T to make up one rung. C always joins with G to make a rung. A little bit of DNA could look like this.

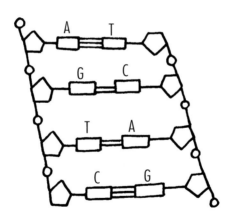

These four bases are very important because they make up a code.

Be a Genetic Scientist
GET CODE-CRACKING

Here's an example of a code.
Can you decode the secret message?

20 8 9 19   9 19   1   3 15 4 5

˙ƎᗡOƆ∀ SI SIH⊥ :spɐǝɹ ǝƃɐssǝɯ ǝɥ⊥

Codebreaker: Write out the alphabet and then put numbers under each of the letters. The letter "A" is 1, "B" is 2, and "Z" is 26. Then all you have to do is to read the letter above each number in the code to be able to read the message!

Can you decode this message? It's easy when you know how to break the code.

8 15 23   20 15   3 12 15 14 5   1   19 8 5 5 16

Powerful Proteins ....

All the different proteins that your genes tell your body to make are made up of small building blocks called amino acids. There are twenty different types of amino acids, and they can be put together in any order. Different proteins are made up of different amino acids in different orders.

amino acids

The DNA in all your cells has instructions about every protein that your body will ever need to make. Because different cells only need to make proteins for their own job (stomach cells only need to make proteins that help them digest food, for example), they only have to read the part of the code for that particular protein. DNA has markers that show the cell where each bit of coding for the different proteins begins and ends. When a cell wants to make a new protein, it finds the beginning marker for that protein and makes a copy of the protein's DNA code. This can then be sent out of the nucleus and given to the protein-making factories in the cell, which are called ribosomes. The job of making the DNA copy is done by a special worker called RNA (ribonucleic acid) polymerase. We'll call her Poly for short.

How Does the Cell Read the DNA Code?.

Poly goes to the portion of the DNA that is coded for the protein that needs to be made. She takes out a large pair of scissors and cuts the rungs in half so that she can pull the ladder apart.

Then Poly gets inside the ladder and walks along the letters.

Snip

snip

As she comes to each letter, Poly writes down what it is and sends out for a copy of the letter that will join with it. Remember, A always joins with T, and C always joins with G. So if she comes across a letter T, she asks for a letter A. If she finds a letter C, she asks for a letter G. Poly strings the letters together as she goes along.

This string of letters is called messenger RNA, or mRNA for short. This mRNA is a copy of the protein code on the DNA.

When Poly has finished copying all the letters in the portion of DNA for that protein, the DNA joins together again. The mRNA copy is then sent out of the nucleus to the protein-making factory.

The DNA code that Poly has to copy can be thousands and thousands of letters long. Sometimes she makes a mistake.

Now, I'll just put in this T...

When she does, the code is wrong, and when the mRNA is sent to the protein-making factory, the code cannot be read properly. This means the protein might not be made properly, and it won't work. This is called a mutation.

Be a Genetic Scientist

SEE HOW DNA CAN BE COPIED

You can see how copying DNA works by making your own model of DNA out of pipe cleaners and modeling clay.

WHAT YOU'LL NEED
- ◎ pipe cleaners
- ◎ four colors of clay—red, yellow, blue, and green

WHAT TO DO

1. Lay out two pipe cleaners side by side. These are the sides of the DNA ladder.
2. Twist other pipe cleaners around the first two pipe cleaners to make rungs, like this:

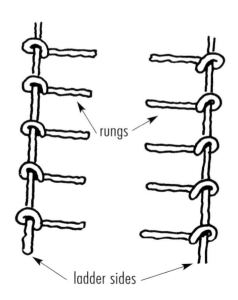

rungs

ladder sides

3. Make up a code for your DNA. Our example will be TTACGT.
   - For every letter T, put a blue blob on the left side of your DNA chain.
   - For every letter A, use a green blob.
   - For every letter C, use a yellow blob.
   - For every letter G, use a red blob.

   Great! One side of your DNA is ready.

4. Remember that A always joins with T, and C always joins with G. So, on the right side:
   - Next to every green blob, put a blue blob to join the rungs together.
   - Next to every red blob, put a yellow blob to join the rungs together, and so on. This is the piece of DNA that your DNA polymerase can copy.

5. Pull the two strands of your DNA apart, just like Poly does, and write down each color blob along one strand. It doesn't matter which strand you're going to copy.

6. For each color blob, find the blob that will join with it. Thread your blob onto another pipe cleaner. At each blob you come to, do the same thing.

WHAT HAPPENS?

Whichever side of the DNA you've decided to copy, you get an mRNA pipe cleaner with blobs that are exactly the same as one strand on your DNA. You have made an exact copy of the DNA code.

Inside the Protein-Making Factory..........

Think of the ribosome as a round building full of workers called tRNA.

Here's what tRNA looks like. Each tRNA worker has a pronged head that only recognizes three letters. It has a supply of only one amino acid.

The string of mRNA is pulled slowly through the protein-making factory, three letters at a time.

As each three letters go through, all of the tRNA workers line up to see if their heads match the letters. When a worker does match the three letters on the string, he takes out one of his amino acids and lays it down.

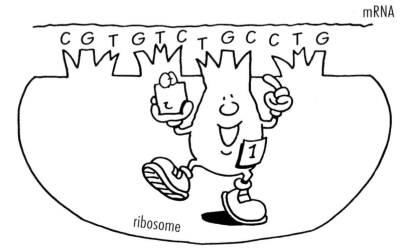

mRNA

ribosome

When a match has been made, the string continues to be pulled through the factory until the next three letters are lined up. The workers try to match themselves up again. The worker that matches the code lays down his amino acid and attaches it to the first one.

After thousands of amino acids are joined together, a protein is made.

So now you know how a DNA code works!

CHAPTER SIX

TO CLONE OR NOT TO CLONE...?

Every cell has a complete copy of the DNA code that tells an animal everything it needs to build its body.

So, in theory, you should be able to take any cell from an animal and let it grow into a new animal, the way an embryo does. But cloning animals is much more difficult than this.

Problems with Cloning Animals.............

As we have already seen, cloning bacteria isn't difficult. It isn't hard to clone plants either, as we'll see later. But it *is* hard to clone animals. This is because there is a difference between the DNA in animals and the DNA in plants.

In animals, something strange happens when the embryo starts to grow. Cells that started off by looking the same as each other take on different jobs.

All these cells look very different from each other. Not every cell has to make every protein the creature

needs. For instance, when a cell becomes a stomach cell, it doesn't need to make the protein that gives you blue eyes. When a cell becomes a hair cell, it doesn't need to make muscle protein. Not only would this be a waste of energy, but it would also make you look very strange!

Once a cell takes on a job in the body, it can't change into a different type of cell.

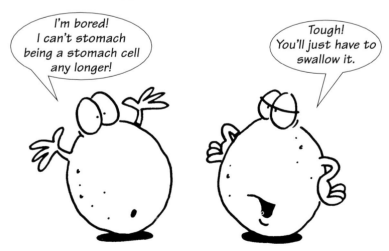

I'm bored! I can't stomach being a stomach cell any longer!

Tough! You'll just have to swallow it.

The DNA that a mammal's cell doesn't use is shut down. Each cell only uses about 10 percent of the DNA code. This is why it's difficult to clone an adult animal. You can't just take any cell from an animal and grow it into a new animal, because some of the DNA will not work. All the genes will be there, but not all of them are switched on.

Some very simple animals can grow new parts of themselves if they are damaged. For instance, a legless lizard can make its tail drop off if it is grabbed by a predator. Then it just grows a new one! Starfish can do this with their arms. Unfortunately, humans cannot grow new legs and arms if they lose them, because the cells have taken on special jobs and cannot change.

In plant cells, the DNA is different. In plants, a cell can switch its DNA back on and become a different type of cell if it wants to. This means you can take a cell from any part of a plant and grow it into a completely new plant—a clone!

Be a Genetic Scientist
CLONE A PLANT

Cloning plants is easy. You may have done it before without even realizing it.

WHAT YOU'LL NEED

- a plant
- a flower pot and some soil
- rooting powder—you can buy this in a garden store
- a glass or clear plastic bottle
- water
- a pair of scissors

WHAT TO DO

1. Pick a side stem growing off your plant and cut it close to the main stem.

2. Dip the stem in the rooting powder.

3. Fill the bottle with water and put the stem in it. Leave it for a few days, and you should soon see roots growing.

4. Fill the flower pot with soil and plant the stem.

5. Keep the stem wet, but don't over-water it.

6. The stem will grow into a new plant with exactly the same DNA as the first plant. You've grown a clone!

Trickier and Trickier—Cloning Mammals

You can clone plants, bacteria, and even frogs. But mammals are the hardest animals of all to clone because their babies grow inside the mother's body. This all has to do with giving the embryo food.

◎ A plant embryo has a food supply in the seed, which keeps it fed until it germinates and grows into a plant.

◎ The embryos of amphibian animals such as frogs have a food supply in their eggs.

◎ Mammals get their food from their mother, which is why babies have to grow inside their mother's womb (uterus) before they are born.

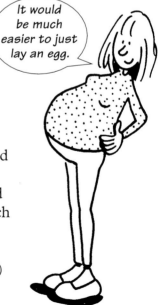

It would be much easier to just lay an egg.

The embryos in mammals create a special organ called the placenta, which attaches to the wall of the mother's uterus. The other end is joined to the embryo's stomach through the umbilical cord. This is how food travels from the mother to the embryo. (When you are born, a doctor cuts the cord off. This is what makes your belly button.)

Although cloning animals is very difficult, it could prove to be very useful. Here are some of the things the technique could be used for in the future:

- making medicine
- saving extinct species
- growing organs for transplants

MAKING MEDICINES

Some diseases are caused when our bodies don't make a protein that they should.

In hemophilia, for example, the proteins that allow blood to clot (harden into a scab) are not coded properly by the person's DNA. If the hemophiliac is injured, he or she can bleed for a very long time—and could even die.

To fight genetic diseases, scientists could make a copy of the gene that codes for these proteins. If they put the copied gene into a cow, for instance, the cow would make the protein in its milk. Clones of these cows would become a medicine-making herd.

SAVING EXTINCT SPECIES

Many species of wild animals are close to extinction (dying out completely). Scientists are now using cloning techniques to try to reproduce the giant panda, so the world won't lose it forever. If this works, hundreds or thousands of pandas could be cloned.

GROWING ORGANS FOR TRANSPLANTS

Sometimes organs, such as kidneys, lungs, hearts, and livers, can stop working properly because of an illness. An organ from a person who has died can sometimes be transplanted into someone with organ failure. But finding replacement organs is very difficult. First of all, the organ from the dead donor has to be undamaged. Second, the transplant has to be performed very quickly.

Even once the transplant is done, there can be problems. White blood cells go around your body destroying invaders and infections. They recognize anything that doesn't belong to your body—including someone else's liver or kidney. The white blood cells will attack the donated organ.

The only way to prevent white blood cells from attacking the transplanted organ is by giving the patient drugs that stop the white blood cells from working. If they don't work properly, they can't hunt down *any* bacteria that get into your body, so you can get sick very easily.

Soon scientists might be able to take a cell out of your body and clone it to make any new organ they want. Because it would be a copy of your own liver or kidney, it wouldn't be attacked by your white blood cells.

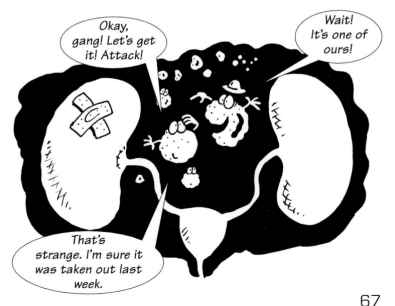

Can Cloning Cause Problems? ....

Some people are scared of cloning. They fear that if scientists can clone a sheep, they could also clone humans. Dr. Richard Seed made the headlines in January 1998 by announcing that he was working on cloning a human being. He said his work was "the first step to becoming one with God." There will always be scientists who want to clone humans, and sooner or later, someone will probably succeed.

A Novel Idea

Cloning humans particularly scares people who have read a science-fiction book by Aldous Huxley. *Brave New World* is about a future where different types of humans are grown in bottles. Each type has had its DNA altered so that it can do a certain job. There are leaders, superintelligent people, normal people, and mutant people, who are used for doing all the nasty jobs, such as cleaning sewers.

If cloning humans becomes possible, people might want to clone dead relatives or famous rock stars. They might even want to clone themselves so they can live forever. Think about it: if a woman cloned herself and carried the new baby in her own womb, the baby would be the twin of its mother, not have a father, and be the daughter of her grandfather!

One of the scariest things that might happen with human cloning is people growing whole copies of themselves. They might keep them in a storage shed and use them for spare parts!

So, cloning could be very useful to us, but it could also be very dangerous. We'll have to be very careful about what we do with it.

CHAPTER SEVEN

THE HISTORY OF CLONING

You may think it's only very recently that scientists began to clone animals. But believe it or not, they started to do it at the end of the nineteenth century. Because animal cells have partially shut-down DNA, scientists could only clone animal embryos. Animal embryos aren't as hard to clone as adult animals because none of the DNA in the embryo cells is shut down.

Animal Cloning Experiments, Part I
Switzerland, 1896

This is Hans Spemann.

He's got a bad lung disease called tuberculosis. He's had to go to a special hospital for the winter, and he doesn't have much to do. He's forgotten to bring along any exciting novels to read, and Nintendo hasn't been invented yet. The only book he has is one about embryos. He decides to do an experiment.

Spemann gets some fertilized eggs from a salamander—an amphibian that looks like a frog and a lizard.

He waits until the egg divides into two cells, and then he separates the cells using a hair from his newborn son.

Each of the two separated cells grows into a new salamander. They are clones of each other.

Warning!
Do not read the next part if you are squeamish.

Spemann tries to do his experiment again, but this time he doesn't split the two cells properly. A weird thing happens—the cells grow into a two-headed tadpole!

The Next Step....................................

Spemann thought there must be a way to clone an adult animal. He thought about growing a cell from an adult animal by putting it inside an egg.

Eggs are very special cells. They have only half the DNA of other cells. Sperm also have only half the amount of DNA. When a sperm and egg join together, they have the full amount. The egg can only grow when it has this full amount of DNA.

It takes two, baby!

Spemann thought that if he took the nucleus out of an egg and put in the adult animal cell instead, the full amount of DNA from the animal cell would allow the egg to grow into an adult animal.

Nope. By the time someone did manage to grow an animal by putting an adult cell inside an egg, Spemann had been dead for a long time.

Animal Cloning Experiments, Part II

The United States, 1952

This is a scientist named Robert Briggs. He took the nucleus out of a frog egg and then took a cell from a frog embryo. He put the cell into the egg, and the egg grew into a tadpole!

So Far, So Good..............................

Briggs and other scientists found out that tadpoles could rarely be cloned this way, and frog cells could not be cloned at all. Why? Because the cells had taken on a job and shut down some of their DNA.

The only way scientists were going to be able to clone adult frogs—or any other animals—was if they found a way to turn switched-off DNA back on. Nobody had a clue how to do this, so most scientists continued to work with animal embryos.

Even though they couldn't yet clone adult animals, scientists were already beginning to get excited about the idea of cloning humans.

If humans could clone them-selves, we could control our own evolution! We could wait until people are 50 and then decide whether to clone them. Then we would get great thinkers, artists, athletes, and beauties. A great person could spend his life from 55 on teaching his cloned children.

J.B.S. Haldane, 1963

Cloning could allow us to fill the world with identical replicas of carefully chosen people.

Gunther Stendt, 1974

Cloning Millions

In 1978 in the United States, someone claimed to have helped a man clone himself.

Writer David Rorvik said that a millionaire named Max had knocked on his door one day and asked him to find a doctor who could clone him. David had agreed to help. He found a doctor, the cloning was done on a secret island near Hawaii, and a baby was born in 1976.

When scientists heard about this, they were furious. Of course, they said, it wasn't possible. But the book Rorvik wrote about this story became a best-seller and made him lots of money.

Scientists knew the story about cloning a human couldn't be true. So far, they had only managed to clone a very young frog embryo, and even that had been tricky. Making a cloned mammal egg cell attach to the mother's womb would be extremely difficult.

In 1984, just as scientists were beginning to give up hope, Steen Willasden managed to clone a mammal embryo. He put nuclei from a sheep embryo into sheep eggs. Two lambs were born in 1984.

Scientists still couldn't clone an adult. The cells from the sheep embryo hadn't taken on a job, so none of their DNA had been shut down. To clone an adult animal, scientists would have to discover a way of making adult cells get all their DNA working. This is what the scientists at the Roslin Institute in Scotland managed to do. They took cells from an adult sheep, put them into sheep eggs, and in July 1996, Dolly was born!

How did they do it? Let's find out by cloning a sheep ourselves!

TIME TO CLONE AN ADULT SHEEP

Are you ready? Then let's get cloning!

Step 1 ....

First of all, take some cells from a sheep. The cells that were used to make Dolly came from an udder. But you could take any cell from anywhere in the sheep. Aside from red blood cells, the only cells you can't use are eggs or sperm cells, because they have only half the DNA needed.

udder

Step 2 ....

Now make sure the DNA in the cell is not switched off anymore. There is a very simple and clever way of doing this. It involves something called the cell cycle.

The Cell Cycle

The cell cycle is a series of stages that a cell goes through when it is dividing into two new cells.

Right after a cell has split in two, there is a short delay while each cell checks that it has all its DNA. When the check is done, the cell begins to grow.

Hmm, this seems fine. OK, you're clear to grow again!

When the cell has grown, it gets ready to divide again. Because each of the two cells will need a full set of DNA, the cell makes a complete copy of all its DNA.

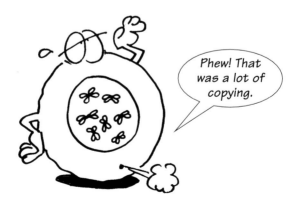

Phew! That was a lot of copying.

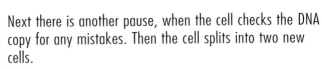

Next there is another pause, when the cell checks the DNA copy for any mistakes. Then the cell splits into two new cells.

Hnnnn!

Go for it!

But sometimes the cells have to rest. This usually happens when there isn't enough food for a cell to divide. The cells need food to give them energy to copy their DNA so they can split in two. If there isn't enough, they decide to stop dividing and take a rest.

Give us a break! I'm starving!

Now this is the important part: when a cell is in the resting stage, all its DNA is switched on. This means all the DNA in a resting cell can work.

But how can you make cells rest?

This is actually very easy. You just don't give the cells any food. You starve them.

Cells in the laboratory are grown in a special liquid called cell culture liquid, which has all the things they need to grow (like the Jell-O you grew your bacteria in). If you take most of the food out of the liquid, the cells stop dividing and rest. This saves their energy. It also means that none of their DNA is shut off anymore.

Step 3 ....

So, now you have an adult cell with all the DNA working properly. You need an egg to put it into.

In sheep (as well as all other mammals), eggs grow in the ovaries. The ovaries have thousands of eggs in them, but they cannot all be fertilized. One egg at a time gets ready to be fertilized and is then sent out of the ovary down to the womb.

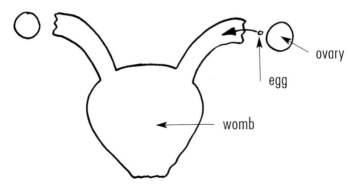

You can increase the number of eggs ready to be fertilized by giving your egg-donating sheep some hormones. The sheep can then be put to sleep and have its eggs removed in a simple operation.

This sheep won't miss a few eggs!

Step 4 ....

You now have an egg whose nucleus has some DNA in it. It's only half as much DNA as a normal sheep cell, but you need to take this out.

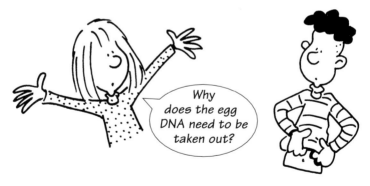

Why does the egg DNA need to be taken out?

The DNA gives the animal instructions about how to grow. If the genes in the udder cell are added to the genes in the egg cell, there will be too many genes. Things would go wrong, and the animal wouldn't grow properly.

How Do I Take the DNA Out of the Egg?

You will have to use a microscope to see what you are doing. Hold the egg steady using a glass rod. Then gently push a syringe into the egg and very carefully suck out the nucleus. Easy!

Step 5

Now you've got an egg with no nucleus and a cell that you can clone.

Get the cell nucleus out the same way you've just gotten the egg nucleus out.

Put the cell nucleus into the egg.

Your egg is now ready to grow into a new sheep.

Step 6 ....

You need another female sheep to put your cloned egg into, so that it can grow into a lamb. This sheep is called a surrogate mother. It is best to use a surrogate sheep that is a different color than the sheep you're cloning. That way, you can prove the lamb is a clone.

Put the egg into the sheep using in vitro fertilization, or IVF. "In vitro" is just a clever way of saying "in a test tube." It means you've fertilized an egg in a test tube and you're now sticking the egg back into a body. This technique is often used for human couples who are finding it hard to have a baby.

IVF is quite simple to do. Extract the egg with a long syringe. Then put the syringe into the sheep's vagina, go up through the womb, and into one of the fallopian tubes. Then squirt the egg out.

The egg moves down the fallopian tube and back into the womb. By the time it gets there, it is ready to make a placenta, and can attach itself to the mother sheep. Then, all you have to do is sit back and wait for your cloned sheep to be born. Congratulations!

CHAPTER NINE

THE FACE OF THE FUTURE

As you now know, cloning is a tricky, intricate procedure. Lots of things can go wrong. For instance, the egg is very tiny and easily damaged. Even the smallest syringe is very big compared to the egg. You have to be very careful about where you stick it, because a damaged egg will die.

Another problem with cloning is with IVF. Getting the cloned eggs to attach themselves to the mother sheep is very difficult. It doesn't happen very often. To make Dolly, 277 eggs had to be used. Of the 277 eggs that had the nucleus from an udder cell put into them, only 13 developed into embryos. Those 13 were put into sheep, but only one managed to grow.

So, if you are going to clone sheep, you have to be very, very patient.

Where Do We Go from Here? ....

In July 1998, scientists cloned twenty-one mice using the same method that was used to make Dolly. This proved that this way of making clones really works.

If we can now clone any adult animal, how far can we go? Could we clone ourselves? And what about *Jurassic Park*, where dinosaurs were cloned? Could we bring back extinct species?

Can We Clone Ourselves? ....

The simple answer is yes! In fact, now that we know how to clone adult sheep and mice, we can clone any living animal on Earth. Human eggs have already been cloned twice, but both clones were destroyed before they developed into an embryo. Some countries are passing laws to stop scientists from cloning humans, because it is such a terrifying thing to do. But because some scientists want to become famous—and might be paid a very large amount of money for cloning—it's probably only a matter of time before a mature human clone is made.

Can We Clone Dinosaurs? ....

Probably not. And it's a good thing, too, if what happened in *Jurassic Park* is possible! Who would want velociraptors roaming the streets?

In the film *Jurassic Park*, a scientist found mosquitoes in amber. These mosquitoes, like mosquitoes today, got their food by sucking blood out of animals. Imagine a tiny mosquito sucking the blood of a dinosaur. It goes to rest on a tree, but disaster strikes. The tree trunk is damaged, and sap runs out. The sap engulfs the little mosquito and kills it.

When the tree sap hardens, it turns into a kind of rock called amber. Millions of years later, the amber is found, still with the fly perfectly preserved inside it. (If you look at amber, it often has little flies inside.)

The idea in *Jurassic Park* was to take the blood out of the mosquito's stomach and find the dinosaur DNA in it. The DNA could be copied and put into an egg without its nucleus. The egg would grow into a new dinosaur.

This sounds like it would work, doesn't it? But there are lots of problems. First, the amount of DNA you would get from the mosquito would be so small that it would be hard to do anything with it.

Then, even if you did get enough DNA, the mosquito could have sucked the blood of lots of dinosaurs. All the different dinosaur DNA would be mixed up. This would make a very strange-looking dinosaur!

The biggest problem is that DNA can break down into lots of different pieces. It can also be damaged. In *Jurassic Park*, bits of DNA were combined with frog DNA to make up any missing parts. But we don't know how much DNA dinosaurs had. There could be a gene missing for something very important! And how would we know which pieces went where?

So, bringing back the dinosaurs doesn't look possible at the moment. But, if cloning humans was thought to be impossible only a few years ago, who knows what might happen in the future? Maybe you'll become a genetic engineer and lead the way. Good luck!